Amazing Change

Poetry of Healing and Transformation:
The Wisdom That Illness, Death, and Dying Provide

by

Robert Carroll, M.D.

Foreword by Perie Longo

BOMBSHELTER PRESS
LOS ANGELES

ISBN: 0-941017-86-9

Cover photo art courtesy of David Meltzer
Layout & design: Alan Berman

Bombshelter Press
www.bombshelterpress.com
books@bombshelterpress.com
PO Box 481266 Bicentennial Station
Los Angeles, California 90048 USA
Printed in the United States of America

The Kalahari Bushman likens a good story to the wind because it comes from far away and we feel it. Such is the case with Robert Carroll's poems. Sometime during the day, maybe while taking a shower or walking the dog, the gorillas of Robert's "Amazing Change" will seep back into my consciousness, and I feel it. All the poems in this collection have that kind of time bomb effect.

—Lawrence Spann, PhD., Editor of *Poet Healer* and *Blood on the Page*

Robert Carroll, physician poet, suggests healing through songs of suffering and a lyric sensibility. His students are already familiar with his prose introductions to poetic surprise; and now there will be even more who appreciate the candor and passion of those surprises. Each poem brings us to important realizations about healing and the mysteries we share as healers and as healed.

—Rabbi William Cutter, Emeritus Professor of Hebrew literature, Hebrew Union College-Jewish Institute of Religion

This book about wisdom brings to life a poetic voice. It springs from the lived-experience of a healer who, like many healers in all wisdom traditions, uses poetry as a vehicle to take us into a sacred space, where we gain the power to remain cool in the eye of a storm. Dr. Carroll puts in plain words how to take on the thousand and one challenges of life and hands over a medicine for life to heal us when we are confronted with illness, death, and dying.

—Kykosa Kajangu, PhD., Author of *Wisdom Poetry*

You'll find in this collection poems that are tightly crafted, poems in form, and poems that burst into Whitmanesque song. Robert Carroll's poems capture all that is the healing nature of poetry and its power to transform the sorrows of human experience. Despite the sorrows and losses of this life's journey, the poet can still proclaim in the closing poem "as I sit at my desk / and gaze out the window / I feel grateful / for all I have left." Healing indeed.

—Mifanwy Kaiser, founder of Tebot Bach, Literary Arts Organization

Dedication

To my wife Susan and son Joshua—
three eggs making omelets

and

To my teachers Jack Grapes and Deena Metzger

and

To all my patients, family, and friends whose stories
inspired many of these poems.

Foreword

I FIRST HEARD ROBERT CARROLL read his poetry in 1998 at a Santa Barbara Cottage Hospital's Psychiatric Grand Rounds presentation. I was awed by his steady and confident presence, his poems full of grit and courage that tackled the most difficult of life's passages: birth, illness, death. I introduced myself afterwards, and told him about the National Association for Poetry Therapy, and invited him to the upcoming national conference. He came, and we have been colleagues and friends ever since, in the business of helping others find themselves through their voices, to discover what Walt Whitman once said, "I am larger than I thought . . . I did not know I held so much goodness."

Over the years I have read many of Robert's poems and heard him read frequently in formal gatherings as well as sitting around a table, when he will just "out" with one from memory. He continues to amaze and surprise with how he handles his material, whether writing about his huge love for his family or compassion for his patients, who "bleed" internally. As a psychiatrist, his poems reflect the soul of a man who himself has lived inside pain and knows how to sit with it and hold another's.

Robert is a storyteller, and he loves to fill you with the details because he knows they will resonate with and reflect your own life, and you both will learn something, transformed in some way. *Amazing Change* is about the breath in and the breath out, and the people we love who change us, and even those who don't, those who are lost who help us find ourselves, and the space where words are born. Robert writes in that place, where you will feel not so alone.

Perie Longo, Santa Barbara Poet Laureate
Author of *With Nothing behind but Sky: A Journey through Grief*

Preface

FIFTEEN YEARS AGO I went through a series of concurrent
catastrophic life events including the terminal illnesses and
deaths of my father and a close friend, the illnesses and deaths
of several patients, the terminal decline of my golden
retriever, and my own undeniable mortality when I had a
skiing accident and needed reconstructive knee surgery. I
began writing as a way of dealing with the inchoate, yet
overwhelming, feelings I was experiencing. I wanted to find
the words to say it, and thereby make the experiences real to
me, and hopefully, to facilitate a healing process for myself. By
writing these poems and sharing them with other poets and
writers and hearing their voices, I came to understand that
what is most personal in the human voice is also most
universal, and that the writing and reading of poetry could
facilitate healing, growth and transformation by expressing the
wisdom that illness, death, and dying provide. So, in addition
to healing myself, I was healing in a community of people who
lent their voices to the universal chorus—the universe of
poetry.

Robert Carroll
Pacific Palisades, CA

Acknowledgments

Some of the poems in *Amazing Change* have been previously published in literary journals including *Spillway*, *Rattle*, and *ONTHEBUS*. Many have appeared in the author's chapbooks: *The Southland* (2004); *B+* (2000); *What Waiting Is* (1998); *Poetry Vulgaris* (1998); *SlamJam* (1998); *Cherish* (1997); *Night Games* (1997); *LA LA* (1997); *InTheVisible* (1997); *Malibula* (1995); *Not Guilty by Reason of Insanity* (1995); *A Boy from Brooklyn* (1994) (all by InCorpus Press); *The Art of the Brain* (Robert Carroll, editor, 2004); *Simple Gifts* with Mifanwy Kaiser, et al (1997); *Alphabet City* with Jerry Quickley and Gabriel Cousins (1997); and *Call and Response* with Mifanwy Kaiser (1996) (all by Bombshelter Press).

Others have appeared in medical journals and books including *The Journal of Poetry Therapy* (Routledge 2006); *eCAM* (Oxford University Press 2005); *Making the Impossible Difficult: Tools for Getting Unstuck* (Thorana Nelson 2003); *Journal of Medical Humanities* (Springer 2001); *Second Opinion* (University of Iowa Press 2007).

My heart rouses
  thinking to bring you news
    of something
that concerns you
  and concerns many men. Look at
    what passes for the new.
You will not find it there but in
  despised poems.
    It is difficult
to get the news from poems
  yet men die miserably every day
    for lack
of what is found there.

from "Asphodel"
by William Carlos Williams

Contents

Amazing Change

Amazing Change

We can go through amazing changes
when we are faced with knowing
we have limited time.
After one woman got brain cancer,
she decided what she wanted
was to go to Africa
to see the gorillas.

She and her husband and the guides
began the long trek through the jungle
up the mountains, but the woman was
having trouble. The guides tried
to convince her to go back,
but she wouldn't.
She struggled and struggled.
Eventually she won the guides over,
and everyone was rooting for her,
but there came a point.
She couldn't go on,
                    so
she lay down on the grass,
and when she did, the gorillas
came out of the jungle
to her.

Being the Stone

I want to be the stone
     and tell
how she held me
in the palm of her hand
rolled me between her fingers
slipped me into her mouth
tasted my salt
tumbled me around.

Then she ran her tongue along my edge
and rubbed my cool body across the scar
     of her breast
put me in her pocket
took me home
gave me to her daughter—
     a special gift.

Mefather

I rose in his wake.
A dream passed
my eyes, my father
lying still
in his tub.

I throw my arms around him
shouting, "Daddy, wake up!"
Bubbles are bursting everywhere.

The Sense

Do not look up to me my child
For heights seem out of reach,
And looking up will make you lose
The sense of what I teach.

The answers lie within us all,
But I looked outward first.
Horizons lend perspective when
Our problems seem the worst.

Delusions grow as people age,
And fail to realize
That growing up is nothing more
Than knowing your own size.

So don't be scared of heights or
Depths that trap us with their lies.
A parent's love is straight ahead
And level with your eyes.

What I Want

What I want is not words
but where words come from—
the space within breath
that calls out our tongues

I Didn't Want to Write Today

I didn't want to write today.
I didn't want to write
I took Ben to the vet today
lifted him into the back seat
and laid him down.

I didn't want to write
the man in the blue scrub suit
put Ben on the gurney and
wheeled him in through the back door
not the front
where all the others held their dogs
on their laps or on chains.

I didn't want to write
the little green room on the left was
where we spent our last few minutes together
or that the doctor told us it was time.

I didn't want to write
it was easy to find the vein
and the liquid was blue
and when the doctor aspirated Ben's blood
into the icy blue anesthetic
death became purple
and in ten seconds he was gone
a breath long and deep
and then gone.

And I didn't want to write
Susan thought it was peaceful
as I watched his eyes sink.

And when his breathing stopped
the air left me too
and the tears stung.
That's when I thought of my father
whose road's the same
whose path's the same,
down and up and down.

And when we took the long ride home
we could still smell Ben in the back.
His fur blanketed the back seat.
And when we got home in the late afternoon
I opened the door as I always do
and I checked for messages,
but there weren't any, so
I told Susan I'd meet her upstairs
and I went to the garage
and got his dish
because it was late
and time to eat
and I forgot he was
dead.

And I thought, who can I call now?
And again I thought of my father.
Then I heard his voice,
It'll be all right, boy, he said,
I know it hurts,
but it will be all right.

B+

When I went to college, my girlfriend said
I don't love you anymore.
I would have given anything to find the words,
    but instead
I smoked a cigarette.
I wrote my heart out in freshman English
    and got a D
    in red.
Overly emotional, the professor said.
I just shook my head and tried to be
    more objective.
I wrote about lunch in the cafeteria, but I was still
    over involved.
I got another D.
Next time I described a bagel
    in two hundred fifty
    words.
For that I got a B and then a B+

and that's where I stayed.
I've been B+ all my life.
Baseball
    bowling
        shooting pool
elementary
    junior high
        medical school.
I'm even a B+ psychiatrist.

People come to me after their child has
    hung himself in the shower
      or their brother died from a seizure
      or their father deserted their mother

or they can't get themselves out of bed
or they don't have sex
or they do
  but not enough
or much too much
or their marriage is cracking up
or their marriage is hanging by a thread

and I be with them
and I help them not
    be alone
our history
      our resource
          our family
             our voice
we live it all
by blood and choice
medication helps sometimes
people do use drugs
mothers do not only love

we all have bodies
    and use them
we all create
    illusion
the father who deserted
    is frightened
his daughter is boxed
    in a corner
her mother defies
    a demon
today is another day.

My Grandfather's Clock

He gathered us
all around him
and asked us each
what we thought:

"I don't think so, Papa."

"Even if you survived the surgery, Sam,
what would be left?"

"No, Papa."

"No."

"The doctor is right, Papa."

"Go, Dad.
Be with Mom.
It's time."

"O. K.," Papa said,
"then it's over.
It's time to say goodbye."

And so he did
to each of us,
and Thursday night
he died.

A-Frame

When my parents were here last week,
they were walking different.
My father still offers his arm
as he always has
but now he leans a bit
against my mother.
Otherwise he'd dodder.

It's sweet
seeing them from behind.
He uses her for balance,
she leans against him
for solidity.
They're more of an A-frame now:
a stable way to build.

Cherish

It's been a year since my friend, Ruth Ellen,
died. The memorial service is today at Hillside.

My father is scheduled for surgery tomorrow.
They're replacing the clogged artery in his leg
with a vein graft, also from his leg.
The incision will run from his groin
            to his foot.
If they don't replace the artery
the toe will turn gangrenous
and he could die from infection.
If they cut off the toe
the stump may not heal
from the lack of circulation
            so
they have to replace the artery first
and the artery in the other leg
can wait for now
but it will need replacement too
if he lives.

My father called the other day.
He told me a story about a man
who owned a one horse shay.
The axle broke
            so
he took it to the blacksmith
to have it repaired.

The blacksmith told him it would cost as much
to repair the axle as it would to buy a whole new wagon
to which the man replied,
            "Well,

if that's the case, then they should build them
so all the parts break at once."

"That's what's happening to me," said my father.
"I feel things closing down and falling away
and I wonder if it means I'm dying?
That that is what dying is."

I told him what Ruth Ellen said when
she was closing down, getting ready to die.

"I'm shedding like wings...
beliefs, relationships...
all falling."

"Yes," he said, "maybe it's the same."

What Waiting Is

(after Philip Levine)

We sit on the bench in the hospital corridor
next to the cafeteria, and we wait.
You know what waiting is.
If you know anything, you know what waiting is.
It's not about you. This is about
illness and hospitals and life and death.
This is about the smell of the disinfectant
that hits you in your head.

In the bathroom you look in the mirror.
What do you see?
Your father's sad face?
Your mother's eyes?
You catch the water cupped
in your thickened hands, splash it on your face
and hope against hope you can wash it away—
the aging brown spots, the bags,
the swelling truth of waiting.

So you go back to that bench.
Maybe your mother is there or your wife
who is waiting for your father who is waiting
for the news from the surgeon
or the morphine for the pain
or the nurse who cleans bedpans
who is waiting for her shift to change
while another man's hand clamps white as a claw
to a clutch of bed sheets, and you wait.

So you hear the news,
and you take the long trip back from L.A. or Detroit—
wherever you're from—

and you see the faces of the drivers
as they approach you out of the fog
and you see this one:
a woman hunched over the wheel like your mother
and you think, *It is my mother.*
And you want to tell her everything
how waiting kills and what it does to your life
that fifty years of marriage is an eyelash blink
but she's past you now and headed in the wrong direction
so you wait.

Then, out of the corner of your eye
you see your father's face in the driver's seat
of a '49 powder blue Pontiac sedan.
The thin sliver of his moonlit profile's smiling
but the nose is too long, and it's not really him
and besides, he'd never understand anyway—
this impatience, this anger, this rage, this love
this fog on the windshield
never even knowing if it's inside or out—
because his whole life was waiting
and what does a fish know of the water
or a bird of the air?

So you push the leaden accelerator down
and act like you're headed to some small emergency
and you don't give a damn about the cop waiting
behind the billboard or death over your left shoulder
and you think you might want to pray
and you do pray, but you don't know what for
and, anyway, you're driving, so you go back
to the endless lines of headlights and traffic
and exit signs until you get home to see the light
flash on your answering machine
but you don't pick it up.
Instead, you go to the bathroom.

You take a shower, take a piss
pull out a carton of leftover food—anything—
but it's cold and you can't swallow it.
So you push the button
and it's your sister's voice
but it's choked
and she can't speak.

That's how I learned that the waiting was over
that my life had changed forever
that this end was a beginning
but I didn't know for what.
I used to think it was death I was waiting for
but that's not what this is. This is life.

So you show up and do the work
and love who you love, and you learn to wait
and if you're lucky, you learn what waiting is
and what you have to give.

This Much

When the boy asked the man
How much do you love me?
the man went down on one knee
then he leaned towards the child
and opened his thick arms
as wide as the earth
until his hands were behind him
and, like Atlas, the world rested
on his shoulders and back.

At the funeral home
before the cemetery
I asked to see my father's body
even though the Rabbi said
I would not recommend it.

It laid in a black walnut casket
in a room behind drapes.
When they opened the casket
I saw it dressed in a shroud.
A hood covered the head.
I wanted to see it, but
the director said
It is not recommended
but Susan and I insisted
so they undid the tie.
His face was pale white.
I ran my finger down his cheek.

After the eulogy
the Rabbi asked me to speak.

I said, "The measure of a father is not only
how much he loves his children,
but also how much his children love him."

I have a picture of my father on my refrigerator
holding his grandson, Daniel.
You can see my father beaming as he watches Daniel sleep.
Twenty-five years ago that baby was my son, Joshua.
Twenty-five years before that, he was me.

During our last night together
I kissed my father on the cheek
and turned to go
but then I turned around and kissed him again.
Then we flew home, and that night he died
so we all turned around again.

In the night between the coming and going
I stood at the side of my bed
with my suitcase laid open.
I saw the shirts, underwear, pants
socks, belts, and ties, and I couldn't remember
whether I was packing or unpacking
or for where
or why.

Then, back in Tennessee
the other pallbearers and I
carried his casket to the grave
and lowered him into the ground.
Then each family member in turn—
I was first, then Susan, Josh, Bonnie, Roy, Nancy
and the rest—except for my mother who couldn't—
each threw a shovel-full of dirt.
The earth went *thud*
as it hit the black walnut.

Later, Daniel, who is three now,
asked his mother why we threw dirt on Papa Joe?
Then he asked his father why are we sad?
Then he asked Joshua
why we laugh when we're sad?
So we told him,
"When you love
you feel it all,"
and we showed him
the world
on our backs.

The Proof in the Pudding

When last I left my friend Ruth Ellen
the surgery to remove her frontal bone
left her with a step on her forehead.
When we went out, she wore hats.
Today I'll visit her in her room.
The tumor is no longer
benign.

In her head
in her eye
in what now appears to be
the end of her life
is my life.

It's the end game.
What a relief to know
all that is left is to live.
Time becomes pudding
pudding air
thick and everywhere.
These are the best times of our lives
these pudding days of grace
when gardens are our guide.
They finally took her eye.
Don't mind.
They finally took her eye.

When I arrived at the house
her daughter Molly gave me a hug.
She'd gone slightly stiff.
I walked in and looked out the back window
at the garden, beautiful and overgrown,
wet with new rain.

I almost missed her in her chair
at the table, sitting there
eating avocado
sliced and laid out flat.
She looked cute
in her bonnet and patch.

"Well," she said,
"except for the eye
and the headaches,
and there are still decisions to be made,
I'm fine."

And it was her all over again
fine in the face of it—
crabgrass roots deep—
fine in her chair
a bonnet and patch
white like cotton
not hospital white
not bleached white
milky white like her
and we settled into our love
for one another.

Oh carry me wind for I am air
she's gonna lose her hair
she's gonna lose her hair
and hibiscus's blooms
and hummingbirds' wings
and deep dark earth held our future
as we shared the last bite of avocado.

Ruth Ellen rose and retired to bed.
Her black cat wanted to come
under the covers after licking Ruth's plate.

I read them poetry.
We all tempted fate.

"What's that beeping?" I asked.
Her daughter appeared out of habit
and unkinked the IV.

"You and Susan and Josh," Ruth said,
"all wonderful, all full,
all richly gifted.
I am gifted too, but unrealized.
I always wanted to write.
I always wanted to paint.
A friend brought me a journal.
I don't know if I'll write.
I don't know if I can.
Whenever I try,
it seems distant or removed."

"You can," I said.
"We will write poetry together.
You must start with your own spoken voice
which is alive here and now:
your house, your garden, the crabgrass, a bloom
the light playing through the leaves
the mud that kept you company in the living room
the last bite of avocado, creamy and green
a friend, your bonnet
the beeping IV
Molly, kinked by your arm
the cat, black and close
everything rich and full
and scented with you.
This is your poetry.
This is your life.

The End Game

I'm slipping, Robert.
I'm sorry I didn't call back sooner,
but I'm slipping, call me.
Her voice trailed off my machine
just before the beep.

I went to the house to her room.
Her face looked like a pumpkin,
swollen, red, and round as a plate.
Her left eye was gone.
She didn't wear a vanity patch anymore.
I kissed her on the cheek.

"I'm closing down," she said,
"getting ready to die.
Sometimes it scares me.
I'm shedding, like wings.
Sometimes I come out whole;
sometimes it's an onion.
Maybe I'm emerging.
Sometimes I feel it.

"No, those are the wrong words.
It's not nothing.
It's something else.
You know me, Robert,
I don't get all mystical,
but something's happening.
I'm shedding from the inside.
It's all falling away—
beliefs, relationships—
all falling.

"I know you're there if I need you,
but mostly I just want to sleep.
Dying's no big thing anymore.
It's a way to go."

Afterward, We All Sat Around in a Circle

After the service, twenty stayed.
A woman in a navy-blue suit spoke first:
"I remember," she said, "when my mother died.
It was six months after we first found
the lump.
Between the breast surgeries
and the metastases and the strokes
she was gone.
I yelled, 'Do it now, Ma! Die now!'
but it took another month."

Then a man:
"Sometimes they need to know
it's O.K. to go.
My Dad was in a coma for weeks.
He got agitated and made sounds, but he couldn't talk.
The doctors said there wasn't much they could do.
'He's terminal,' they said.
'We'll just give him morphine
and make him comfortable.'
But my brother said, 'No, not yet.'
And he and my sister and I
got together and agreed
it was time for Dad to go...
so I was chosen.
I sat on the edge of the bed.
I said, 'Dad, It's O.K. to go.
We'll be O.K. without you.
It's all right,'
and I said it again and again
and I swear he heard me
because in thirty minutes
he was gone."

Then a woman in her sixties:
"It's been nine years since my son died.
I was so passive...
I got him into the hospital—
I had to fight for that—
but when the doctors told us to leave the room
because they had to change the dressings,
I didn't say, 'No, I'll stay!'
I just went ... like they said.
I couldn't do him any good like that.
Then, when I was out of the room
his heart stopped.
Nine years it's been.
I don't think I'll ever forgive myself."

A man in his forties:
"My brother ... he's paralyzed.
He's in a wheelchair—
a gunshot wound when he was sixteen—
He takes care of our Mom.
He does it all.
He washes for her.
He cooks.
He cuts watermelon.
He's a blessing, he is.
I just can't do it.
He blames me, but what can I do?
Some people just aren't cut out for it."

Then another man about my age:
"I'm a little scared to say this,
but I have no story.
I don't cry.
When they're gone, they're gone
nothing more.
I work in the movie business.

People come and go.
We can be close for six months,
work together every day
then it's on to the next project.
I may never see them again.
That's what it was like
when my friend Ernie died
like he's out there somewhere
too involved with another project.
That's nothing unusual for Ernie.
Time just passes.
People say there's something wrong with me.
I don't know.
Sometimes I wonder."

A man in his thirties:
"I've thought about it
been in therapy over it
processed it till I'm blue
but in the end
I still can't accept it.
In the end, she's still gone
no matter how I work it out.
We were fifteen.
I've got children myself now.
I love my wife,
but my sister—
She was all of our heroes—
tall with dark red hair—
She drowned going after a ball.
I saw her go out, and I heard her yell,
and when she went under,
I saw her."

A silver-haired woman near fifty:
"The strange part for me

is thinking about the future.
My cancer was removed ten years ago.
Between the surgeries and the chemo
and the complications,
it was all I could do
to live day-to-day.
Now it's been ten years.
I'm beginning to believe
I have a future.
I've lost a lot of friends along the way,
but we were there for each other."

And so it went
around and around
until we were done.
Then we hugged
and we touched.
Then we left.

And We Call It Skin

My father died by inches—
a cancer excised from his armpit
a stroke in his cortex, dialysis
a heart attack, the amputation of a toe.

"I'm losing my vision," he said,
but try and get him to stop driving.
And of course, I'm the same way.
It's the passivity of the activity—
just the touch of the toe to the pedal—
the last ball of a ball bearing foot on the floor
the whirring of the engine
the big cat covering ground—
he loved those old GM's—
Buicks, Pontiacs, Chevrolets—
the bigger the better.

That's why when the guy who drove down the Pelissippi
        Parkway
rammed into my father, who could say if my father's blindness
was to blame or if the man really did come out of nowhere?
My mother didn't know
as I saw his hollow eyes slow
as if death was the blessing he so
cherished. He was finally finished.
It would be all done.

Until then he was imperturbable.
You could sneak up behind him in the old recliner.
The gravity of the chair made the whole house whirl.
When he was in it, he would not budge.
The house could be swept up in a tornado, but that chair—
a black hole in the Universe of my family life—

was an eye of God that would not be moved,

                              except for the strange sliding
as he pushed himself up and back
gripping the armrests, thrusting his pelvis out—
the last unbridled move I saw him make—
the chair spinning, wisps of tissue blotting hemorrhages
on his face, his shins, his forearms, his surface paper thin
the backs of his hands brown with the breakdown products
of extravasated blood below the pearl
of his outer keratin coat—the boundary
between life and death
in and out
all we know
and we call it skin.

Kaddesh for My Father

(Joel Carroll, born Joseph Cohen)
   (after Allen Ginsberg)

Strange I should go to New York this October night
walk down the Boulevards of Brooklyn
to a wedding on your side of the family
while Manhattan's million incandescent lights twinkle
and I used to think they were stars.

Bob Dylan's new CD scratches in the back—
how the legends fade—hollow eyes not yet closed
as the year plays out. Escape to oblivion's no more
an option—life in L.A., worshiping green.
The real estate market stirs and takes a turn—
appetites whet—I raise my rates.

Strange how potato eyes grow under the Tennessee sky
and sprout as some rooted thing—
you could no longer live on Long Island,
and I salute you.

The red-eye I take on Saturday night descends
into Kennedy. I walk the cobblestone Bowery streets—
bums asleep in doorways—the homeless weren't
even invented back when we went to The Cooper Union—

Shooting pool at Julian's off Union Square—
Brunswick-Balke slate tables—three-inch thick slabs—
enough for a man the size of you—
me not yet a big apple.

Love is a fragile thing—dissolved in tears—
held up by shed wings—my voice—this possibility.
You played basketball against St. John's

when even six feet was tall—
I bowled against St. John's,
and now six feet is everything—
and we both hoisted balls
and reached for some earthen sky—
yours to be in Tennessee—
me in my office, you in my memory—
and how good it is that the lion takes the buck
and still the sun arcs across the horizons of our lives
and connects us through that other ring.

Susan saw a rainbow out the bathroom window,
and it was all to lower my head.

Part 2

Blessed holy
blessed holy
blessed father
blessed memories—

dropping popsicle sticks down
a King's Highway sewer grate in Brooklyn—
I was barely two—
going to the zoo in Rock Creek Park—Washington, D.C.—
we drove through the creek
that flowed across the road—
getting Sniffy-the-dog
you drove a black and white taxi—
buying our first car
a forty-nine powder blue Pontiac sedan—
our next was a '52 Willys—
no one had ever seen fins before—
hitting a home run in the parking lot
of our garden apartment in Anacostia—
I couldn't understand how you could hit it so far—

teaching me to throw a curve ball
behind May's Department store
Levittown, Long Island—
fingers crosswise to the seams—
you made my palm burn when I caught you—
making a ten-pin at the Sunrise Lanes—
cross alley—you were robbed of a turkey
and a two-hundred game—
grinding a six-inch reflecting lens for my telescope
in the basement of our split level in North Bellmore—
I knew the top forty by heart—
Murray-the-K and his Swinging Soirée—
submarine races—
going through puberty.

Tell me, Father, when did you first break?
Was it the marriage or the kids or the cancer
or the depression or the multiple sclerosis?
Was it the job, Dad? Was it the slow steady
decline? Was it the blood vessels breaking
one arteriole at a time?
Did you sell your soul to be a family man?
Did you ever cheat on Mom?
And when at last you were disabled
and fell back into disuse,
was it really a failure of nerve?

I learned about loving from you,
but you didn't know how to see it through,
and you didn't know how to fight.
You only knew how to love and retire.

Father, Father, blessed Father,
your shits smelled like you were king-of-the-john,
and I thought you were deep as you retreated
behind locked doors and open books.

Was there no peace?
No one ever knew what you wanted
until you were ready to die.
Joshua and Susan went back to the store three times
to get that Sony dual-deck stereo boom box
with recording option, and you said,
"I never had a present."
Who would have guessed?

Dad, we loved each other,
but there was never much passion in it.
I had to get that from Mom.
She's doing all right.
I cut out a picture of you last Tuesday
and carried it around in my pocket.
It felt good to have you there.

Psalm

My father who art in Tennessee heaven,
hallowed in name
hallowed in memory
hallowed in cloth
peeping out behind shrouds,
your strong arms hoist me to the sky
where I peer wide eyed,
"Look, Dad, Coney Island."

Holy blessed father, yes,
though I walk through the valley
of the shadow of your death,
your smiling face comforts me.

Yis-ga-dal vi-yis-kad-dash sh-may ra-baw.

Blessed father, sacred father,
you gave your life, your paychecks
your ravaged kidneys, your scarred retinas,
your heart. You gave us your heart.

Blessed are you in the house in North Bellmore
Tho' you couldn't make the stairs anymore
blessed in Tennessee
blessed in the ground
blessed in your diabetic multi-system failure
blessed in University Hospital
blessed in the vein graft that replaced your femoral artery
blessed in the surgery scar they cut from your groin to your
        foot
blessed on dialysis
blessed at your blessed microwave
        in which you heated the blessed liquid
        then ran it through the blessed tube
        into your blessed abdomen,
blessed in your amputated right big toe,
blessed in the suit against the podiatrist that cut you.

Yis-bor-ach, v'yis-ta-bach, v'yis-po-ar,
v'yis-ra-man, vi-yis-na-seh,
v'yis-ha-dor, v'yis-hal-leh, v'yis-ha-lal,
sh'ma d'ku-dah-sho, b'rich hu.
Blessed are you my father,
v'yim-a-roo, Aw-mein.

Part 3

Oh, father, what have I left out—
the inertial guidance system you designed
        for the Atlas missile?

your thick cock?
the workbench you built in the basement?
the desk in Nancy's room?
the string sculptures you fancied and made
        for everyone?
the smell of you crawling from your armpits
        hunched over the workbench
        sweat dripping from your chin
        your hairline receding
        your belly hanging over your belt
        hairs growing out of your nose?

You taught me to shave,
to comb my hair by dousing it with water—
to part it on the left—
to tie my tie, my shoe laces,
my tongue.

You took me to the deli, and we watched
        the surgeon slice lox,
then you let me order the bagels and rolls.

What have I forgot?
Your forehead, furrowed and deep?
Your ugly clothes?
What were you thinking?
What am I?
Your eyes.
Your eyes saw the Brooklyn streets
        with horsedrawn wagons.

Adored by your sisters,
you were Uncle Yacey in Yiddish.
When I saw Aunt Laura's eyes last month,
you were there too, watching.
Your spirit.

Praise to your spirit, Father,
      and to you who watched
      and tried to never let us fall too hard.

Part 4

Praise to the yapping yelping call of the dogs.
Yapping yelping yawps praise the call of the dogs,
call call, whistling wind,
call call, calling, come.

Yellow dogs and black birds speak.
The children are asleep,
but they stir to the sounds of sirens
and the neighborhood dogs.
We do not live on these rooftops any longer.
Clotheslines no longer stretch between neighbors.
Only the black birds and the yellow dogs make sense—
this yawp, this call, this paradise:
    Caw caw caw caw
    caw caw caw

And another car makes its way up
      North Jerusalem Road,
headlights casting shadows on the walls
      of my darkened room,
then up and away as the pitch of its swish passes
then lowers then fades:
Shhhhhhhhhhhhh
Shhhhhhhhhh
Shhhhhhhh

Happy Man

Just the other day
I was sitting on my sofa
looking out over the canyon
thinking about my life
     my work
     my loves
     my friends
and I rolled back and kicked
my feet and hands in the air.
Like a baby I grabbed for everything
and everything I wanted I had right there
on the couch. I was a happy man,
and I knew it.

Later it was still true
and into the night, the same.
"I'm a happy man," I said.

That night, when my *yes's* followed hers
and we made all the moans
we lay quiet and stroked the long lines
of our animal bodies, and it was good.
I've come into myself in my fifties, and all I know is
I showed up, did the work, and started Prozac.
I'm a happy man.

Night's Enfolding

As day turns toward evening
the blue yellow light dims down
and the world turns to golden.

Then iridescent orange
falls off into darkness as we slip
into night's enfolding.

I Have a Secret

I have a secret
I keep from myself.
It's not a bad secret.
It's more like when you don't
throw your arms around someone
and tell them you love them
or you leave a piece of meat
on your plate because you don't
know how to stop the hunger.
     So,
I go back to the silence
behind the words
and I smile the smile
I see in the morning
after I brush my teeth
shave my face
and take my pills—
wash them down with a swig of water—
and wait for them to work.

Reflection

Can I be me inside you?
Who are you so deep?

I saw the sea the other day—
not from the breaking shore—
but from below
where all is still and
closes in my madness.

The Graft

It's been three months post-op
and rehab is progressing.
My knee's still a little gimpy,
but the ligament seems strong.
It's an allograft, not an autograft.
An autograft would have come from me.
An allograft comes from a cadaver.
So, I have a dead man in me.
At least I used to think it was a man,
but it could have been anyone.
I might have a little woman holding my knee together—
perhaps a German.

A friend of mine gave me an article
on German mortuaries and morgues
that sell internal body parts like meat.
Of course if the technicians were allowed
to sell internal body parts wholesale like meat for cash
it probably would have been a foreigner or a dark one.
I might have a Pole or a Pakistani holding my knee together.
A big Sudanese longshoreman—that's what I want—
someone who used that knee, but didn't use it up.
And I hope they died young.

I wonder what happened to all those Iraqi knees?
There must have been a million Iraqi knees
available for the plucking.
But what if it was one of our boys
your daughter, my son?
I don't like that idea. It's too alive.
I don't want a live man in me,
I want a dead one.

A live one might cry out in the middle of the night—
a spasm of agony lying dying on some field of honor—
Perhaps a woman slaughtered fresh by friendly fire.
Maybe she'd be nursing her baby.
But the baby's knees would be too small for me—
but the woman—if she were tall like my mother
or supple like my wife
with good strong knees and muscular thighs
that can hold me tight in the night when I cry out in pain,
We are losing the children!
Good strong knees. That's what I want!

Meat

I didn't expect the abdomen to splay open
    with the single drawing of a blade
    or to see so far inside
    that the pumping of blood
    was just work.

I didn't expect the boy to strangle himself in the shower
    or the girl to blow out her brain with dust
    or the father to burn his children with a frying pan
    or the woman's gastrointestinal tract to die
    or the Hawaiian princess to be brought back to life
    when I suctioned her throat to breathe for her
    smashed her chest to pump for her
    slid needles into her wrist to hydrate her
    walked down the hall, I released her.

I didn't expect this raw meat
    to be the meat of my life, but
    I am a witness.
    These are my eyes.

Poetry Vulgaris

DATELINE AUGUST, 1997—from the brochure:
   The Eighth Annual National Poetry Slam and
   Connecticut Poetry Festival—For five days in
   August, 156 poets from 33 teams from all over
   America and the world will assemble in
   Middletown, Connecticut to read and compete
   and host workshops, open mikes and poetry slams.

If I told you how Jerry almost missed our plane
and we all about shit in our pants
or how at the Nuyorican Café in New York
hundreds paid to hear us slam
or how the audience rocked
as our voices lifted off into air
would you think
Man, there's no poetry there.

If I told you in Cambridge
we went up against the best
and we all kicked butts
till there weren't any butts left
and the words rang out over burgers and beer
and all the buzz going round was
Yeah, L.A.'s here.
Would you still think
that's not poetry you hear?

If I told you we invaded like insects from Cleveland,
Chicago, Worcester, San Francisco, and Sweden,
London, New York, and Providence too—
even Germany invaded—
so what else is new—
would you still turn your skeptical nose?
Would you?

And if I told you my colored skin crawled
all black-american-latino-asian-red-golden-brown
like sugar molasses running down
running down running down
would you still doubt me
or my sincerity?

So I took hold of the mic, and I tilted the stand
and my father—dead and gone—came alive in my hands
as poet after poet gave it up to be just another voice
in Whitman's great collectivity
for this love and glory
this dignity and respect
this poet to poet
this head to head.

Day after day we slammed face to face
poetry to poetry, grace to all race.
Renegade, Patricia, Beau Sia, Da Boogie Man—
Deborah Edler Brown won the haiku slam—
Haiku, erotica, street songs, exotica
voices from Middletown rang out the land
and I could hear our forefathers and mothers all stand
and grab the mic with both of their hands.

I heard Whitman, Neruda, and Langston Hughes.
I even heard Miles blowin' out blues.
Santa Fe, San Jose, Kalamazoo—
One poet from Detroit sounded like Maya Angelou—
And we sprang up like new grass
and spread like wild fire
in this glorious August spring of our lives.

And I swear, even Willie Shakespeare was there
and The Bard be so bad he banged out a **ten**,
but Da Boogie Man was even more awesome

so some judge gave him an **eleven**.
And as the sweat poured down my head
and drenched my skin,
I was awash in it—
poetry—
stinking like life and common as shit.
Now if that's not poetry,
I don't know what is.

Not My Boy

(after Patricia Smith's "Undertaker")

I know a girl who writhes like Saint Vitus.
She dances arms waving
eyes rolled up in her head.
She prays to some other God.

I know a boy who is dying
not in his body but in his mind.
He's dying, scared he's dying.
He knows. He sees.
The trees appall him now.
His father watches in horror
as he takes pills from jars
eyes big as knotholes.

In the fifth-floor room
of the Neuro-Psychiatric Institute
the boy lies strapped to a bed.
Arms legs chest flail
eyes wild
spittle whips the air.

The nurse draws the medication
into the plastic syringe
flicks the barrel for bubbles
then tests the plunge.
She shoots the ether deep
to enshroud his mind
and spread it against the sky.
There was no way to stop
his headlong leap into madness.
His engine hot brain will burn cooler now.

His mother says, "This is not my boy,"
and collapses her face in her hands.
The nurse puts her fingers on the boy's head,
"It will be all right," she says
and puts a Band Aid
over the injection site.
"Nooo," moans the mother,
"Where is my boy?"

Then, "Here," she pulls out a picture of her boy
strapping, handsome, full of hair.
Then, "Here," another in a football jersey, and
"Here," another at the prom
his sweet smile spread
his angular body cocked
his girlfriend's on his arm.
"What happened to my boy?"

So I tell her about brain chemistry
and the angel dust we found in his blood
but she is not listening; instead she is rocking
eyes wide, arms clutched to her sides.
So I change the subject
to insurance and the bill, because I know
if I don't get something up front
the hospital will exhaust the coverage
and collecting will be hell, so I tell them
if I could just have the first fifty percent
as the boy lies sleeping strapped to his bed
and I, dead tired, fold the father's fat check
and make my way down the long green hall
to the girl who dances
all of us up long past our time
and under my breath I thank God,
Not my boy.

Sometimes the Blues

Sometimes the blues is all there is
    black blues
    brown blues
    white girl mo-joing
some down home way
of whispering to your heart
that old suitcase of despair
your finger tap tapping on your knee
at the bus terminal
public in a way all identity is stripped
your lips now willing to let it pass.

Sometimes the blues is
your face in your hands
elbows on your thighs
the surprise of nothing
going nowhere
silence moves
disconnected thoughts
the clock ticks
all the poetry's lost.

Sometimes the blues is the death of a child
grief runs wild—the *Why my child?*
The blues is forever
the heart breaks
never again
takes its place.

Sometimes the blues is me. I'm alone.
Sometimes the blues is we, you're at home—
time and space estrangement
custody arrangements

always the saying, *You did what?*
Sometimes the blues is what is not.
Sometimes the blues is all you've got.
When the blues becomes what
you've got nothing left to lose,
then the blues is the news
and the news runs through you.

We are all out on the dance floor
the rhythms of living
in pelvic thrust
electric air hair flies
women slung low
the sub-bass beats
the underside of audio
big mirrored balls riot
life's fractured rays
men pump arms raised
pray to the scatter of light
the shatter
the right
the glory of horns
a sax blows low alto
booze and ooze
the secretory miracles of women
the cocks slide side to side.

The flat of my palm guides her hips
pursed lips
hands fanned
the spirit is among us
we're anemones in its current.

Let It Come Natural:
A Conversation with the Lunatic Raymond Means

Back in the day, and I'm talkin' 1967, 1968, 1969,
it was Vietnam time, and I was a medical officer
in the United States Public Health Service
stationed at St. Elizabeth's Hospital in Washington, D.C.
in the heart of the country on a ward for criminally insane
        men—
the domestic front lines.

One day I went to the ward to do sick call.
I heard that my patient, Raymond, was locked in seclusion
after he threaded a coat hanger up his urethra
to try to perform a therapeutic abortion on his bladder
because, as his note to me said,
I was inseminated by the Guard called Dog.
But I had no idea what that meant
because Raymond was crazy
but he was that special kind of crazy
where the truth sometimes finds
itself.

> *That's right,* said Raymond,
> *just come on in through the front.*
> *Don't be no back door man.*
> *My name is Raymond*
> *and I'm the one in charge.*
> *You want to know who's in charge,*
> *see who carries the keys.*
> *Me, I'm here for protection.*
> *¿Como se llama, mi amigo?*
> *¿Como se llama?*

Raymond was naked
except for a blanket draped over his head.

There were feces smeared on the walls
and the guard told me Raymond had just finished lunch.

See, here's the thing.
We got astronauts, right?
They land men on the moon, right?
I'm an extraterrestrial explorer too.
So what's it to you if I complete
my own food chain loop
and eat a little of my own poop?
Call it an experiment in living.
I'm a poet.
I smear shit all over these walls.
It's all about truth.
It's all about what's news.
Let it come natural, Doc.
That's the title of your first book
Listen, you're a writer, right?
So take this down.
Some weird shit happened
on the ward last night.
You know that dick, Dog?
Well, Dog was taking a taste of Raymond'ses shit
when out of nowhere
in walks two policeses with mattresses,
and they start beating on Raymond'ses head—
and I'm seeing red, when the big yellow dude
with the corkscrew doo says, 'How am I supposed to live
when I gotta be lying on top of you?'
Then he gets all purple and red and his face explodes
and I can see the cum start bubbling up in his throat
and he's got this shit coming out his mouth
and he's got this zit on his forehead
and I can see it's just beginning to ooze
so I say in my best high stylin' dialect,
'sweetheart, I just love it when you're hard.'

Then I squeeze the shit out of that pimple.

Well, he must've been some kind of homophobic mutha fucka.
You see this nick?
I needed five stitches.
Tell me, Man,
how am I supposed to live?
I pay taxes.
I voted for El Presidente.
¿Como se llama, Man,
como se llama?

L'Chaim

A man lifts a boy in the air
his hands up under the boy's belly.
The boy's eyes go wide
wide as his back-arched smile.
Bubbles are bursting everywhere.
The man is gone now, and the boy who is me
is as old as my Grandpa Hymie was then.

Grandpa didn't get to see my boy born
did not get to see him grow up to be a man
who stamps out metal in a sheet metal plant
so his body will feel the feel of a worker's back
the revolution of his mind
and the march of history.

Capitalism makes us into replaceable cogs
not like my father or the boy who is me
lifted wide, big as the sky
the man's hands on his tummy
tickling his vision of yesterday's meal:
left-over chicken, yams, and peas,
and the quease of a life
on the line.

If I had to do it over again.
If I had to lie with my face in the dirt
and learn to play on broken knees
and eat that second helping
of chicken, yams, and peas
I would take the time this time
to lift my head up, keep my eyes open
play more, and chew slower.
I would look at the mud of my father's grave

and let memory carry me in his wake.

Yes, the bubbles are bursting; the boy is me;
my son is lifting the world on his back
and I, hobbled on wounded knees
on this brick earth
faced with the world of one live child
—We are lifting each other—
play the play and write the songs
and remember the wonder of *why*—
eyes big as the world is wide—

but I will never go back.
Yet I see the patterns through leaves and trees
dissolve and resolve the blue L.A. sky
the burnt terra cotta earth
and the too-true green of *terre verte*
and I say to you, I see it all
and miss it
all.

A Trip to the Third Street Promenade

It started as soon as the valet took my car
in front of the Broadway Deli—a beggar.
His sign said, VET.

It is said in the Passover service that
when Elijah comes, he will come as a beggar.
It is said that the measure of a people is
if they would take the beggar in
as they would take in Elijah himself.
Only then will we be free.
So shall we be judged.

I hand the VET a dollar—
my standard feed.
He's a good beggar.
He doesn't need to say anything.
He just is.

The woman standing five yards further away
tries to foist flowers on me she's cut
from the gardens of neighboring homes.
She only shows me one eye.
She mocks me. I walk past.
We have a relationship.
We don't like each other.

I came tonight to read poetry at The Midnight Special.
I came to read this poem though it is not yet written.
Tonight the beggars are here for me.
Rain begins to fall.

I find shelter in the doorway of an artifact shop.
An old man in dreadlocks stands in the corner.

I nod and smile. He nods.
His teeth are white, his skin is blue.

I say, "Father, I have been looking for you."
Now he smiles. I drop a five in his box.
The flower lady is throwing chickenfeed to the pigeons.
She calls them by name: *Beatrice, Herringbone,
Bedlam.*

I make my way up the promenade
and check my wallet for singles.
I have three left to give
plus the five I just gave
plus one for the VET
makes nine. Nine bucks
and I haven't even finished
this poem.

After reading, I walk back.
The man in dreadlocks is reading a book—*Hamlet.*
He says, "Go speak to your mother, there."
He points to the flower lady,
one eye peering from under her shawl.

"My mother?" I say.
"Yes, Boy. She is mother to us all,
and she is not happy. Go speak with her.
Tell her your secret. Tell her how you feel.
The play's the thing that makes things real.
If you want to be free, you must both be
and want to be."

I walk towards her.
"Mother," I say, "forgive me for not being the one."
"The one?" she replies.
She unfocuses her eye, then,

"Yes, yes, why did you leave me?"

"You delivered me into the world, Mother,
and the world is my home."

"And where has it gotten you, Boy?
Where? Do you ever call?
I spit on you, for all you've done.
Here, buy a flower for your wife.
Now she's the one.
Take the bird of paradise.
Only five dollars
to help an old woman."

"Five dollars for a flower? Mother
I would rather just give you the five."
"It's not the flower," she says,
"It's the cost of paradise that's high."

Fire in the City of Angels

It's that time of year—
Fall, Halloween, the Day of the Dead—
the time when we are most in touch with
the world where trees call our names.
At night the souls that inhabit the garden of stones
congregate. Fires throw shadows in relief
on the landscape. The trees dance.

It is a time of fire in Southern California.
It hasn't rained all summer, so an offering
must be given to appease the gods of winter,
the nature of desire—
FIRE! FIRE! FIRE!—
the rip—
flames fan the hillside.

Two hours to evacuate.
Decide, decide—
Papers, photos, files—a picture of a child—
Grab some blankets. Pack a case with clothes.
Layers.
We don't want to be cold.

The firemen drag their hoses over the scorched earth,
faces black, eyes swallowing visions.
Another house goes up fanned by the Devil Winds.

           Water.
Water is dumped by helicopters on to the advancing flames.
Retardant dropped by cargo planes falls out of the sky—
    the stench of charred flesh—
    a horse got caught in barbed wire—
    DESIRE! DESIRE! DESIRE!—

A thousand homes aflame and counting
a woman, almost eighty, shrieks.
She and her husband built this place
had a family, raised the kids
while here on network television
their daughter, Sally, scans the ashes
for treasure, finds golf clubs
three of which have not melted.

We will not sleep well tonight, the air awash in ash—
    the cloud of smoke hovers over L.A.—
    the wish to douse myself in water—

Never has a night been so long
as the visions of yesterday morph into tomorrow
the spirits in the trees sing their songs.
The future holds we are not alone
as the souls congregate in the garden of stones
and the fire in The City of Angels burns on.

Dr. Bob's Psychomedical Poetics—Infomercial 1

Ladies and Gentlemen:
It's Dr. Bob's psychomedical poetics
the only *no problem* way to write poetry from and thru your life.
You say you got no life—*no problem*
Dr. Bob is both a poet and a psychiatrist
You say you don't like poetry, and you never heard
of psychomedical poetics—*no problem*—
You can trust Dr. Bob.
He's a real doctor.

Everything you need to know is contained on his cassettes.
No hard to get off shrink wrapped casing on these CD's.
In just a few short weeks instead of wishing you had a life,
you'll be writing from and through the one you've already got.

And with Dr. Bob's methods, everything's easier.
Got a problem with your mother-in-law? *No problem.*
Solve it the Dr. Bob way—write about her.
Have it published in national magazines.

Got no balls? *No prob-*
lem. Write Haiku, whip own sor-
ry ass into shape.

Made a pact with the Devil?
We want details.
And with Dr. Bob's methods
there are no nasty side effects.
(Of course Dr. Bob's mother didn't speak to him
for months after what he wrote.)

Contained on every CD are Dr. Bob's methods
to release your voice by unleashing your tongue.

Did you know that the largest section of the human brain
        controls the tongue?
All language based species communicate in tongue.
Survival itself is predicated on being able to suck, lick, taste
        and articulate.
Among humans, poets have the biggest pre-frontal lingulae
        on their brains
and lingula in Latin means tongue.
Alan Ginsberg is reputed to have lingual gyri
        as big as walnuts
and Maya Angelou's are huge.

So, people, release your tongues
so they may snap like whip or snip like scissors.
Tell your truth from the inside out.
Dr. Bob will show you. How?
Here just a sample of what you'll get:

If you want to find your voice,
write like you talk.

What's most personal
is most universal.

It's the poem in the poet
not the poet in the poem
that's important.

The poet puts the reader on the stool,
then gets out if the way, and

fuck 'em if they can't take a joke.
That's right.

Just $19.95. Cash, check, or money order.
Just call 1-800-n-o-p-r-b-l-m. *No problem.*

Or contact us at noprblm@pacbell.net
and remember, you can trust Dr. Bob.
He's a real doctor.

Eileen

Eileen has breast cancer.
The lump was removed last year.
It was chemotherapy and radiation
for the next six months.

Eileen lost weight.
Her skin burned.
She vomited every day.
Her hair fell out—
first wisps, then tufts,
then clumps.

Her daughter couldn't stand it—
she was only thirteen—
seeing her mother
pull out her hair.
"I don't care!"
yelled her daughter.
"I don't care!"

"Wanna pull?" said Eileen.
"Wanna pull out some hair?"

At first the daughter couldn't bring herself to do it,
but her mother cupped her face with her hands.
"I need you, baby. Help me. Take a pull."

So the daughter grabbed a strand,
and it came out easy.
So she grabbed another
and another
then a clump
and out it came.

Then they put on music
and danced
and grabbed hair.

They played Chaplin and burlesque.
Hitler had a funny moustache.
They put sideburns on Jews.
Eileen became a Billy goat.
They bayed at the moon.
When Eileen became bald
they laughed, then they wept.

Then the daughter
pasted patches in her armpits
and a tuft between her legs.

"Look, Mom.
I'm a woman now!"
she said.

Up and down
the women jumped
and screamed
until they were both exhausted
and Eileen's scalp was red.

Then they laughed
and hugged
and went to bed.

Denial

The tumor in his brain
probably came from the lung cancer
in his chest diagnosed last year.
He had his lung removed
and it all seemed clean
but now here we are.

"I'm in two kinds of denial," he said.
"One is *this can't be happening,* and
The other is *I can't do anything about it.*"

He went back to work,
So he'll know who he is.
Otherwise the day falls into itself
too slowly to bear, and
too slowly to know
where he fits
in.

I Wondered

In the middle of life's commotion
Kathy died in her room—
Her last safe place
before The County told her
about the bulldozers

And I saw her sweet face smile at me
in the way that I had to just love her
and I wondered if she did it
with the pills I gave her.

Incest Taboo

(a persona poem)

The taboo is not against doing it.
The taboo is against remembering it
and talking about it.

My parents want me dead.
They never wanted me to be born
and now they'd rather I killed myself.
I'm just a problem ruining their perfect lives.

That's why they can't hear me.
There's no room for
    Grandpa finger-fucked me or
    My father made me suck his dick or
    My uncle came to me in bed and
    slid his hand between my legs.

How do I hate someone I love?
How do I love someone I hate?
How do I make them hear me?
How do I make them want me
      to live?

Optimistic Rag
(a sestina)

I called the nurse to ask about my patient and get some
　　　additional history.
I was going to testify that the patient goes crazy, like an
　　　animal in the forest
she becomes wild, eats what she can find, hides under stoops.
　　　Grave
disability is the legal term. I provide her with treatment. I
　　　prescribe medication.
It calms her, settles her, helps her to see and think straight.
　　　Yesterday, I saw optimism
in her eyes. She was going out on a pass with her priest. She
　　　seemed pleased.

She wanted to be released, but I knew if she were, she'd be
　　　picked up by the police,
and with all the past hospitalizations and incarcerations, it
　　　seemed to me her past history
was against her, and I was going to testify that although I
　　　would like to remain optimistic
being released in a jungle like Los Angeles was a bad night in
　　　anyone's forest
and the only thing between this girl and her being made into
　　　prey was medication
and protection, and the only way she would stay alive was if
　　　someone stood between
her and her grave.

So I will testify that she continues to need supervision, and
　　　that her condition is still grave,
and although I believe she will not agree with me, I also
　　　believe that she will likely be pleased

that I came to support her because she fights for her freedom,
　　but knows she needs medication.
She's a smart young woman—doesn't like to take crap from
　　anyone—you can see it from her history.
She doesn't like drugs whether they're mine or someone else's,
　　and she believes in the rain forest
and its secrets, and even though she has not made much of her
　　life, she's always been optimistic.

And I can see a green flame burning in both of her eyes that
　　brightens like optimism
glows from embers hovering like fireflies above the tombstone
　　in the graveyard
where my father is buried in Tennessee—the greenest
　　state—it's just hard to believe. Forests
betray us when we're lost in the woods. Like animals we roam
　　and are pleased
by small pleasures, soft roots, little treasures, and this becomes
　　our histories
and how we determine who needs care, concern, a house in
　　Beverly Hills, or more medication.

We evaluate all this, make a stew of it, our brains scanning for
　　answers as we medicate
ourselves into some state of preparedness. There's no cause
　　for pie-in-the-sky optimism
when all we've got are the stories we tell, and the possibilities
　　of imagination—the histories
of our lives and times and wishes and desires and the long
　　moments—the graveyards
of our reveries, the repositories of our dreams, and this destiny
　　pleases us, and we are pleased.
"Please, help me," I beg the Nurse. "Please help me sift
　　through this historical forest

for the trees distract me and keep me tied to the underbrush
    wishing for deforestation
wishing for a better earth, the lines of patients awaiting my
    next dose of medication
some screaming from hallucinations, some grinning as though
    they are pleased
with the news they will be locked up at the bottom of the giant
    spiral of optimism
their teeth spread so wide they look like rows of tombstones at
    the graveyard.
We all have a past. We all have a present, and our futures will
    be history.

And just the thought of it—for all the past history,
all the time spent in the forest
all the hours with stones in the graveyards,
all the prescriptions of all the medications
all the patients and families who have come to this optimism
I am pleased.

Associations

Here,
as I begin this sestina,
I swing on my corpus callosum, left side
to right and back in time, and this simple
gift crosses the convolutions of body and mind—
the tightrope walker puts one foot in front of the other—
    associations

to red balls juggled—he crosses the chasm—
    associations—
the twinkle of stars that shine, here
as I peer into space. I don't mind
the pricks and thorns and the unforgiving concrete,
    but the sestina
shows us a way to stay simple, to put one simple
foot in front of the other and be delivered to the other side—

Inside.
"Keep it simple," the man with the cancer in his pancreas said,
    "There are so many associations."
With the news he has less than a year to live, he longs for
    simplicity,
to cook a few vegetables, eat a potato, walk by the ocean, take
    care, be here,
share a few words with someone he loves, write a poem to his
    son, a sestina.
If he could only find the time, it would quiet his mind.

If only his daughter would forgive him instead of reminding
him to wrack himself with remorse for the divorce as his
    insides
betray him. And how will poetry save him now? Not some
    dumb sestina

to express his regrets. "Keep it simple," he said, and he
        associated
me with his family and friends. He said he had come here
to die in Los Angeles close to them with me in attendance.
        It is simplicity

he craves. So we stay with the basics, one foot in front of the
        other—simplicity
itself—We focus on what is yet left undone, and how easy it
        is not to mind
and how time shifts and grows large in small moments, like his
        son now slumped at his desk, here
as he cares for his father's affairs, but is there any way to heal
        the rift with his daughter? Inside
I feel maybe, but maybe he'll run out of time. So I told him my
        associations
to other dyings and how giving things up is a part.
        A sestina

speaks with the voice of necessity, building bridges where
        there is no bridge. A sestina
invites feats of performance and association. The discipline of
        practice makes simplicity
from the complexity of how we bridge gaps. Associations
come: I remember my friend and my father and my dog—all
        dead—and how they serve to remind,
and the tears well as emotion flows from inside,
and the sting that keeps my eyes red is mourning for every
        here

that will one day be gone, while here
        in this poem, a simple sestina
longs to be, and inside
        the rhetoric lies the line, *Keep it simple,*
as I, with him on my mind,
        walk the tight rope, awash in the flush of my associations.

Who Holds the Lollypops

Charlie has become incoherent.
He talks in his sleep.
He may be hallucinating.
No one knows if it's the tumor
or the hemorrhage, or too much morphine.
They drained his stomach yesterday—
passed a tube through his nose—
and he got some relief from the pain
but he's going downhill.

Yesterday, his friend found
that he'd eaten too many morphine
lollypops, but he doesn't remember.
She called hospice, and they're waiting
for a response. She doesn't know
if he'll be able to go to the doctor on Monday,
but if he can, he'll need a wheelchair.
He's too weak to walk.
Maybe a transfusion will help.
Maybe not, but one thing's for certain,
he can no longer hold his own lollypops.

Blood-Streaked Life

How do we know if today is the day
The sun drops out of the sky?
A small bird flies.

The mother dove has mouths to feed.
The gaping babies strain
For regurgitated worms and seeds

They rub her throat with their beaks—
Craned necks abristle—
Until she gives the blood streaked life
Even as the world is open
Even as their eyes stay shut.

Spiritual Soup

To make a good soup is to make a good marriage—
the carrots, the meat, the potatoes—
Each maintains an integrity and each melts into the other.
This communion is the essence of good soup and of good
          marriage.
It's what makes marriage sacred and what makes soup
          married, so
marriage is in. Throw it in the soup.

So is having a kid.
When my son was born and almost died, I prayed.
I'd never prayed before, but it was the only thing to do.
I came to it naturally, through necessity.
Let's throw prayer into the soup too.

I have often walked into a kitchen and smelled
a good sweet and sour cabbage soup simmering on the stove—
flanken so tender you can just suck it in—
and the aroma puts me at home on a shtetl in Russia—
although I've added my own modern touch, which is crushed
          pineapple
and oh my God, it is good.

My wife, Susan, just walked in.
I put my arm around her waist.
I stroked her flank.
She smiled.
She walked out.

And here's another thing.
When I was doing yoga
I felt my whole body move into the poses.
They were integrated.

I was whole.

How can you know where you're going
until you realize what you're becoming?
Ripening is everything.
It's a strange land I inhabit
but at least I feel welcome.
So there, welcome is in.
Put it in the soup.

Another time I felt the spirit was out on the dance floor at
        Harvelle's
moving to the blues. The spirit was among us.
Put that in the soup along with my whole history –
Playing stoopball until dark with my pink Spaldene ball
the death of my father
his slow deliberate decline from diabetes
the same disease his mother had
the same disease I have—
That goes in the soup.
That's the sour with the sweet.

Put my sister's cancer in too.
A good soup can mellow some bitterness
Witness horseradish and turnips.
I called my sister today.
She says she's feeling great
But she's on a new estrogen patch
And she's been energized.
That's what this soup really needs—some energizers.

How about a few good poems?
Let's throw in some Rilke—
    Be fierce, break through
    Then your great transforming will happen to me
    And my great grief cry will happen to you

And how a bout a little Mary Oliver?
What is that wonderful thing that just happened to me?
And Whitman—
I am large. I contain multitudes.

I read some poems to the psychiatric residents today
about families and relationships. They liked them.
Maybe there's hope.
Throw hope in the soup.

My wife's Aunt Ethel used to have a stock pot simmering all
    the time.
When she died someone said they found molecules of soup in
    the pot
dating back to 1945. Excellent,
we'll throw the psych residents, Rilke, Mary Oliver, Whitman,
    Aunt Ethel and 1945 into the soup.

1945 was the year I was born.
My birthday, if you write it out is 1-2-3-4-5—
Twelfth month, third day, nineteen forty-five.
I always thought that was lucky.
Throw it in the pot.
You can always use a little pot luck.

Now we're ready to turn on some heat.
It's O.K. to bring things to a boil initially
as long as you keep the pot stirring to prevent scorching.
Nothing's quite so sad as a good soup gone bad.
Then begins the process of the simmering.
This is where the true marriage takes place.
With my sweet and sour cabbage soup,
It takes about three hours.
I've been married thirty-five years.
After a good long simmering, let it stand.

Then skim the fat and put the soup in the refrigerator
        over-night.
It's the standing, cooling and reheating the next day
that gives soup its depth of character.

So once you've done all that, you have a soup you could
        die for.

You should come to my house some time.
We could read some poetry together
have a bowl of soup
turn on the basketball game.
Before I left my house this morning
I told my wife and son I wouldn't be home for the game.
Susan told me not to worry because she and Josh would stand
        in for me,
but I think I'll cancel my last appointment.
It's a marital therapy, and a good soup will keep.
I could see them next week
And besides, our team is down a game.

The Clown

I know The Clown. He smiles
　　　　but he doesn't laugh.
　　　　　　He takes the cake
　　　　　　　　and puts it in his face.

He is frustrated and pent up
　　　　　　but he can't be angry,
　　　　　　　　not and stay with her.

It's not the sex though he needs the release.
　　　　Wanting to be wanted
　　　　　　drives him to
　　　　　　　　distraction.

Unsatisfied, all there is
　　　　is to shrink away
　　　　　　or blow up
　　　　　　　　a balloon.

On stage, he holds them in the palm of his hand.
　　　　But after, when the sweat
　　　　　　and the pancake come off
　　　　　　　　he looks in the mirror

through the water and soap
　　　　　　and cold cream and hope
　　　　　　　　for one more review.

That's when he sees
　　　　through the layers of time
　　　　　　and the crush of the crowd,
　　　　　　　　his hair's wispy and grey:

He's just another man,
    and he feels
        afraid.

Ground Zero

I dig the earth with my hands
claw stones with my nails,
sift ash through my fingers—
bone and tooth fragments
burnt out by morning
spread on the ground.

The winter rain washes the ash
to the bodies below.
The rotting flesh
the caustic ash
now together
turn to soap.

T. S. Eliot Plays Me Like a Gong

(in response to "The Love Song of J. Alfred Prufrock")

If we drown, we drown
but we do not drown, no.
Instead we go around and around
speaking of Michael
Jordan or Jackson
or some other hero
known to the many
taken in by the most
though not our generous host—
the table is set and yet we try
the possibility that reality
is nothing more than morning toast—
a loaf of bread gone crisp.

Do I dare twirl this wisp of hair?
Do I stare? Do I stare
at the beautiful turn of a thigh?
Do I stare at your auburn hair
your skin aflame in this skin's game?
All the same, I do not wish to indulge
this dish of consummate consumption.
Were it not for the eruption
I doubt I'd have the gumption, but
I do not think anyone begrudges the way
my hair is cut short for my balding pate,
the last hurrah not a minute too late
to think for a moment to stop and wait.

Whitman stopped.
Whitman waits.
Whitman knows
the body electric is where it all goes

into despair, joy, ecstasy, and
I'm not half the man I used to be
if I can't cut the grass in this crass soliloquy
of voice and word and opulent choice
the noise of the highway rising from below
the cars on their way go the ways we all go
down the highway of life, that rocky road
to the bushes to the bushes to the bushes.

Can't you find another time when you is more than you,
when you is me, and we is a chorus of electricity?
We will rise. We will rise
and take with us all the lies
the last great hope to go where we all go—
Michelangelo? I don't think so.

Recently scientists found a black hole
that emits sound fifty-seven octaves
        below middle C—
evidence that the big bang is credible
but more important, that we and everything else
is riding on the pulse of that inaudible sound
undetectable until now, unspoken until now.

I think, perhaps the meaning is in the imagination,
machinations of red wheel barrows and dreams
springtime in the winter, the wish to survive all the lies.

It's time to go backwards.
Let's catch up with the train of our youth
where the lies helped us to survive—
We loved World War II.
Now it's memorialized
in a reflecting pool.

The Washington Monument
shouldn't be an impediment
when what we need is a sacrament,
not all the excrement
doled out by our government.
This genocide is testament
that there is something unwise
in the eyes of The Masters.
Anesthesia's not the answer.

The black holes sound.
Our bodies resound.
If we drown, then we drown.
Turn the tables upside down.

As the evening spreads itself
against the iridescent sky
we will go together
you and I
and together
we will rise.

And Hockney And Hockney And Hockney Who

David Hockney's collages have me atwitter.
David Hockney's collages have me aflutter.
David Hockney's collages vibrate—
the Grand Canyon, the Brooklyn bridge—
his back yard is cluttered with the most curious things
in repetitive patterns—the most curious things—
repetitive patterns—the most curious things.
My eyes flit from frame to frame to frame
to frame the ins and outs, the colors shout out
the floor boards cross and criss, and I'm up on
my toes leaning to see as he sees, my feet below me
the vista spreads out—this canyon, this road, some friends,
a room—as if we have all our eyes at once—
as if we have all our eyes.

Today I sit at my desk at my desk.
The leaves of the tipajuana trees flutter in the breeze.
A hummingbird visits, hovers, and leaves.
A hummingbird hovers and leaves and leaves me looking for
      another.
The violet jacaranda flowers grace the tops of branches
the tops of branches of branches in vertical orientation.
I orient on balance through time
and I'm here all the time—time after time after time.
I see another hummingbird flit.

    Humming,
I write the poem of branches and flowers
and trees and hummingbirds. It's the branches they rest on.
They rest on the branches, then they fly and drink from the
flowers. Drunk from the flowers, they fly off into trees into
trees—
        and me?

I spy Sunset Boulevard winding around the Lake Shrine—
Topanga is off to my right—and the blue Pacific rolls
in rhythms of hammered gold—
These hammered golds anoint this pointillist view
with sky blue sky and the blue sky blue, in thicknesses
even air can't compare to the hammered gold ocean
and the hummingbirds darting above the floor boards.
And Sunset winds, and Sunset winds its way down
and the balance is struck—I am blue. I am gold.
I am hibiscus and tipajuana. I am atwitter
in the leaves on the breeze blowing easy in the canyon.
Hummingbirds hummingbirds hummingbirds light
on branches, and the grass is green green and the sky is blue
     blue
and Hockney and Hockney and Hockney who,
and Hockney who sees, wears glasses like we do

Psychiatrist to Emergency
Psychiatrist to Emergency

I don't treat the bleeders.
I treat the father with bladder cancer
who leaves a note
then jumps off the Santa Monica Pier.
I treat the veteran who gets in your face
on the Third Street Promenade, talking
"How about another mutha-fuckin' dollar,"
and "Satan, the Devil is here!"
You see, the Viet Cong still don't sleep . . .
not in his ears.

I treat the street whore
who gives blow jobs for crack chips
until the police find her unconscious
smiling gagging
on a hunk of red meat
stuck in her throat.

So I tell the father to increase his morphine
because I know that pain can drive someone mad.
Then I explain to his son who repeats it in Greek
to his father who smiles and nods, *Yeah.*

Then the veteran refuses medicine
and punches a nurse in the nose,
so I strap him down
and explain how now
I can give him a shot
whether he likes it or not
as the crack head woman moans,
Jesus!
eyes rolled
jaws locked.

I don't treat the bleeders,
but my patients still bleed.
The father who is dying
now smiles with relief.

The veteran needs his medicine
because more of them have died
by suicide
than died in the entire Vietnam War
and sometimes we all wonder,
what are we fighting for?

But the cracked-out street whore
down on her knees
who had pneumonia and seizures
from undiagnosed HIV—
she knew—
when with Jesus on her lips,
her pimp yelled,
Shut the fuck up, Bitch!
Suck now!

And as her eyes rolled up
she locked her jaw shut
and she seized
Jesus's love
ate his body
drank his blood
ecstatic
with the flood
of her savior
in her mouth.

The Beach of Broken Hearts

On the beach of broken hearts
    lovers lie face to face.
The lagoon swells to overflowing
    with the falling of new rain.
Sand settles under
    the undulations of waves.
Sounds of surf roll
    through my brain.
Gravity takes
    a holiday.
A boy casts a stone
    to the waves.
Iridescent orange and misty pink
    have their way.

I sip my Starbuck's on the dune overlooking the pier.
The stones I collect are all broken hearts
cracked with worm holes
veins of granite
pockmarked conglomerate.

They tell the stories of a million lost kisses—
mermaids rolling pearls in mouths deep with shells.
The ocean swells.

I hold my dear treasure
    clicking broken hearts together.
This one died of fracture,
    that one from decay.
This one's a chevron
    a thousand years in the break.

I want to run up to the lovers
Tell them life is cast in stones
Show them their own
but they sleep on the beach
of broken hearts
together and alone.

Dr. Bob's Psychomedical Poetics—Infomercial 2

Ladies and Gentlemen:
It's Dr. Bob's Psychomedical Poetics—
the only *No Problem* way to write poetry
from and thru your life.
You say you got no life?
No Problem

Dr. Bob is both a poet and a psychiatrist.
In just a few short weeks instead of wishing you had a life
you'll be writing from and through the one you've already got.
And remember, you can trust Dr. Bob.
He's a real doctor.

And with Dr. Bob's methods, everything's easier.
Got a problem with your mother-in-law? *No Problem.*
Solve it the Dr. Bob way—write about her.
Publish it in a chapbook.
She won't speak to you for months.

No balls? *No problem.*
Write Haiku, whip your own sor-
ry ass into shape.

Now let's do some poetry.
First, if you want to find your voice,
write like you talk.

You wouldn't say,
Twas brillig and slithey toves
did gyre and gimble in the wabe.
No one talks like that anymore.
Instead we might say,
Brilliant, that slimey toad Tom e-traded his dot com.

Now he's jazzercizing like a wannabe.
Don't think you can do it?
Do it anyway.

If you say, *The fog rolled in on little cat feet,*
no one cares, but if you say,
I'm sorry officer, but I couldn't see your cat
in all this fucking fog, well anyone can relate to that,
and if he arrests you, write from and through the feelings.

Here's a piece written by one of Dr. Bob's poet patients,
Mr. Billy Bob Cohen from West Hollywood. He came to Dr.
    Bob
with a little assertiveness problem. The piece is entitled

On the Stool with Tiny

I'm in lockup with a serial rapist named Tiny.
There's only one stool, and Tiny wants it.

Now, the beginning poet might write
I feel a torrent of unmitigated rage,
but did Billy Bob do that? *No way.*
He learned Dr. Bob's method—image, moment, detail—
so instead he wrote,

I saw the legs of the stool run from my chest
to the floor as he circled to my rear.

Now that's better, Billy Bob, because it puts you
right on the stool, but check this out,

His erect cock brushed past my cheek.

That's even better because it puts the reader on the stool.

As he waved his kielbasa-sized dick in my face,
I clamped down on his left ball.

(and who hasn't known that feeling?)

Blood spurted into my eye and dripped down my cheek.

Just look at those details, and talk about curing that
     assertiveness problem.
Just $19.95. Cash Check or Money Order. Want to use a credit
     card?
No Problem. And remember, you can trust Dr. Bob, he's a real
     doctor.

April Is the Coolest Month
(after T.S. Eliot and Jerry Quickley)

After winter rains have soaked the earth
and awakened tangled roots, the seeds and bulbs
covered over in the waning days of summer
burst into bloom. Browns become greens
and The Southland again turns golden
hillsides a riot of mustard and nasturtium—
I picked a few and ate them—
as jacaranda, tipajuana, and bougainvillea
all give their love in riots of colors
and the creeks run in the canyons
as the snow-pack melts in the mountains
and the ocean's blues and greens all sing
as poppies bunch on the hillsides.

It is Spring
and all that Spring brings:
daylight savings, endless evenings,
baseball games and income tax
as whales make their way up the coast bearing calves

But somewhere downtown a child hangs her head
because the neighborhood boy shot her dog
in the neck, and the blood oozes black
on the dying dog's back:

All of language is spoken on the out breath
All of life begins on the in.
All of death is spoken on the out breath
All of life begins on the in.

And the beggar woman who collects Styrofoam
in shopping carts in front of the Deli at Fifteenth Street

and Wilshire Boulevard
begs for quarters, her skirts bound around her
scabbed-over legs, an old man takes a bite
of his lox and eggs and thinks about Elijah
who could be the Messiah but appears as a beggar—
the old man would have never recognized her—
Instead he dripped ten drops of wine at the Passover Seder
one drop at a time, one for each plague

drip blood drip drop
drip vermin drip drop
drip darkness drip drop
and the slaying of his first born
drop drip drip drop

and he can hear the *swish swish*
swish swish of the mop
as the busboys slide sidewise
while young men ride in drive–bys
moving to the beat of the pumped up hip hop

don't never stop, don't never stop
don't never never never never never stop

While the old man who emigrated from Germany
reads the numbers on his forearm
in the writing of his enemy.
And as the woman collects her Styrofoam
and the old man knows
that his family's all gone
and the light changes
and the car lurches
and leaves the woman alone
and again it's Spring
in The Southland.

Robert the Dragon

The last days of summer are gone
and the sunlight has toned itself down
to the cold. I want to breathe in
the chill of this day
have my chest open up
fill the air with steam
from my nose.

Yiddle Mouse

On the day we buried him—
his four tiny paws and five-inch tail
curled inside a Minute-Maid can—
we made history. We buried Yiddle Mouse.

My son was barely as tall as the trash can
next to the porch where we dug the hole
the uncomprehending tear on his cheek
the inevitable, "Why?"
the memory of the bird I shot as a child
who came alive in my hands wings flapping
despite the b b gun pellet
that shot out his eye.
Life is more frightening
than death when it awakens us
wings flapping.

Yiddle Mouse in a Minute Maid can—
expired—our son kneeling by his grave
brushing the dirt into the hole
until all you could see was Minute,
and then even that was gone.

My wife and I searched each other in silence—
Who forgot the water, the food?

What Can I Say?

We finished moving all the furniture
switched our bedroom with my office
so now I'm writing in a room with an Eastern exposure.
The sun is streaming through the moats in the blinds.
The trees are different on this side.
Some loom over me to my left while
others step up the hill to the gardens above
and if I stand up and look to my right
there's a crack of ocean sparkling in the sunlight.

The gardeners' lawn mowers crack the quiet with their sputter
and the blues of the sky soften into mist over the water.
The sounds from the parking lot are of a world waking up.
This will be a good place to write.

The bedroom's better too, more ventilation at night.
The ocean breezes make my breathing easier
and the sounds of the traffic from Sunset are only a muffled
        hum
something to sleep to when my mind wanders to oblivion
and the dreams come—

My golden retriever, Ben, walked down a boat ramp into the
        water.
He walked out and down until he was completely covered
        over.
I could see his sweet face look up to me
the surface of the water flat as glass.
He had a mournful look of love
as if he wanted me to know he was all right
but alone, separated from me up above.

And I knew Ben's sweet face told me something of my own,
closed under by life's pressure
but wanting to burst up in the fragrant air
the sweet smells of Summer
Springtime in Winter
the smell of wet hair
tumbling tumbling tumbling in space
where up is not up, where there is no there there.

And the timeless presence of my dog remembered
tells me I still have much to learn from history
because Ben is still with me, even though he's in memory.
And the history of his life had a presence in my own
from the time he was a puppy and I slept with him
to calm his whimpering, to the time he grew into doggy
       adolescence
and got strong like my son. And then he came into his prime
with his flaming golden hair as I stepped into mine with my
       coppery beard
but then he turned gray, as of course we all must—
father to son, rust to rust—
and I felt my decline measured in the life of my dog.
As his hips went limp, my father's legs gave out
and his kidneys stopped, and his heart clogged
and his skin developed hemorrhages that pulled him down.

And Ben, my beauty,
condensed all of our three generations
into his fourteen short years of life.
Then he visited me in my dream
his golden fur glistening in the sunlight.

He walked straight into the water
and when he was below
he looked at me and waited
as he's waiting for me now

to rise and break the surface
or to dive and meet his presence.
The seaweed in browns and golds floats
to the surface and sways in the current.
The spirit is among us.

I am strong. I am free. I am here at my desk
and the Spanish speaking gardeners turn off their lawn
        mowers
and sit down to rest. And it's Summer and it's sparkling
and the breeze sways the branches
and my bedroom is my office
as I sit at my desk
and gaze out the widow
and I feel grateful
for all I have left.